The Vision Of Hermes

Edouard Schure

Kessinger Publishing's Rare Reprints

Thousands of Scarce and Hard-to-Find Books on These and other Subjects!

- Americana
- Ancient Mysteries
- Animals
- Anthropology
- Architecture
- Arts
- Astrology
- Bibliographies
- Biographies & Memoirs
- Body, Mind & Spirit
- Business & Investing
- Children & Young Adult
- Collectibles
- Comparative Religions
- Crafts & Hobbies
- Earth Sciences
- Education
- Ephemera
- Fiction
- Folklore
- Geography
- Health & Diet
- History
- Hobbies & Leisure
- Humor
- Illustrated Books
- Language & Culture
- Law
- Life Sciences

- Literature
- Medicine & Pharmacy
- Metaphysical
- Music
- Mystery & Crime
- Mythology
- Natural History
- Outdoor & Nature
- Philosophy
- Poetry
- Political Science
- Science
- Psychiatry & Psychology
- Reference
- Religion & Spiritualism
- Rhetoric
- Sacred Books
- Science Fiction
- Science & Technology
- Self-Help
- Social Sciences
- Symbolism
- Theatre & Drama
- Theology
- Travel & Explorations
- War & Military
- Women
- Yoga
- *Plus Much More!*

We kindly invite you to view our catalog list at:
http://www.kessinger.net

CHAPTER V

THE VISION OF HERMES [1]

ONE day, Hermes, after reflecting on the origin of things, fell asleep. A dull torpor took possession of his body; but in proportion as the latter grew benumbed, his spirit ascended into space. Then an immense being, of indeterminate form, seemed to call him by name.

"Who art thou?" said the terrified Hermes.

"I am Osiris, the sovereign Intelligence who is able to unveil all things. What desirest thou?"

"To behold the source of beings, O divine Osiris, and to know God."

"Thou shalt be satisfied."

Immediately Hermes felt himself plunged in a delicious light. In its pellucid billows passed the ravishing forms of all beings. Suddenly, a terrifying

[1] *The Vision of Hermes* is found at the beginning of the books of *Hermes Trismegistus*, under the name of *Poimandres*. The ancient Egyptian tradition has come down to us only in a slightly changed Alexandrian form. I have attempted to reconstitute this important fragment of Hermetic doctrine in the sense of the lofty initiation and esoteric synthesis it represents.

encircling darkness descended upon him. Hermes
was in a humid chaos, filled with smoke and with
a heavy, rumbling sound. Then a voice rose from
the abyss, *the cry of light*. At once a quick-leaping
flame darted forth from the humid depths, reaching
to the ethereal heights. Hermes ascended with it,
and found himself again in the expanse of space.
Order began to clear up chaos in the abyss ; choruses
of constellations spread above his head and *the
voice of light* filled infinity.

" Dost thou understand what thou hast seen ? "
said Osiris to Hermes, bound down in his dream
and suspended between earth and sky.

" No," said Hermes.

" Thou wilt now learn. Thou hast just seen what
exists from all eternity. The light thou didst first see
is the divine intelligence which contains all things in
potentiality, enclosing the models of all beings. The
darkness in which thou wast afterwards plunged is
the material world on which the men of earth live.
But the fire thou didst behold shooting forth from
the depths, is the divine Word. God is the Father,
the Word is the son, and their union is Life."

" What marvellous sense has opened out to
me ? " asked Hermes. " I no longer see with the
eyes of the body, but with those of the spirit. How
has that come to pass ? "

" Child of dust," replied Osiris, " it is because the Word is in thee.' That in thee which hears, sees, and acts is the Word itself, the sacred fire, the creative utterance ! "

" Since things are so," said Hermes, " grant that I may see the light of the worlds ; the path of souls from which man comes and to which he returns."

" Be it done according to thy desire."

Hermes became heavier than a stone and fell through space like a meteorite. Finally he reached the summit of a mountain. It was night, the earth was gloomy and deserted, and his limbs seemed as heavy as iron.

" Raise thine eyes and look ! " said the voice of Osiris.

Then Hermes saw a wonderful sight. The starry heavens, stretching through infinite space, enveloped him with seven luminous spheres. In one glance, Hermes saw the seven heavens stretching above his head, tier upon tier, like seven transparent and concentric globes, the sidereal centre of which he now occupied. The Milky Way formed the girdle of the last. In each sphere there rolled a planet accompanied by a Genius of different form, sign, and light. Whilst Hermes, dazzled by the sight, was contemplating their wide-spread efflorescence and majestic movements, the voice said to him :

" Look, listen, and understand. Thou seest the seven spheres of all life. Through them is accomplished the fall and ascent of souls. The seven Genii are the seven rays of the Word-Light. Each of them commands one sphere of the Spirit, one phase of the life of souls. The one nearest to thee is the Genius of the Moon, with his disquieting smile and crown of silver sickle. He presides over births and deaths, sets free souls from bodies and draws them into his ray. Above him, pale Mercury points out the path to ascending or descending souls with his caduceus, which contains all Knowledge. Higher still, shining Venus holds the mirror of Love, in which souls forget and recognise themselves in turn. Above her, the Genius of the Sun raises the triumphal torch of eternal Beauty. At a yet loftier height, Mars brandishes the sword of Justice. Enthroned on the azure sphere, Jupiter holds the sceptre of supreme power, which is divine Intelligence. At the boundaries of the world, beneath the signs of the Zodiac, Saturn bears the globe of universal wisdom." [1]

---

[1] It is unnecessary to state that these Gods bore other names in the Egyptian tongue. The seven cosmogonic Gods, however, correspond with one another in all mythologies, in meaning and attributes. They have their common root in the ancient esoteric tradition. As the western tradition has adopted the Latin names, we keep to them for greater clearness.

"I see," said Hermes, "the seven regions which comprise the visible and invisible world; I see the seven rays of the Word-Light, of the one God who traverses them and governs them by these rays. Still, O master, how does mankind journey through all these worlds?"

"Dost thou see," said Osiris, "a luminous seed fall from the regions of the Milky Way into the seventh sphere? These are germs of souls. They live like faint vapours in the region of Saturn, gay and free from care, knowing not their own happiness. On falling from sphere to sphere, however, they put on increasingly heavier envelopes. In each incarnation they acquire a new corporeal sense, in harmony with the surroundings in which they are living. Their vital energy increases, but in proportion as they enter into denser bodies they lose the memory of their celestial origin. Thus is effected the fall of souls which come from the divine Ether. Ever more and more captivated by matter and intoxicated by life, they fling themselves like a rain of fire, with quiverings of voluptuous delight, through the regions of Grief, Love, and Death, right into their earthly prison where thou thyself lamentest, held down by the fiery centre of the earth, and where divine life appears to thee nothing more than an empty dream."

" Can souls die ? " asked Hermes.

" Yes," replied the voice of Osiris, " many perish in the fatal descent. The soul is the daughter of heaven, and its journey is a test. If it loses the memory of its origin, in its unbridled love of matter, the divine spark which was in it and which might have become more brilliant than a star, returns to the ethereal region, a lifeless atom, and the soul disaggregates in the vortex of gross elements."

Hermes shuddered at these words, for a raging tempest enveloped him in a black mist. The seven spheres disappeared beneath dense vapours. In them he saw human spectres, uttering strange cries, carried off and torn by phantoms of monsters and animals, amidst nameless groans and blasphemies.

" Such is the destiny," said Osiris, " of souls irremediably base and evil. Their torture finishes only with their destruction, which includes the loss of all consciousness. The vapours are now dispersing, the seven spheres reappear beneath the firmament. Look on this side. Do you see this swarm of souls trying to mount once more to the lunar regions ? Some are beaten back to earth like eddies of birds beneath the might of the tempest. The rest with mighty wings reach the upper sphere, which draws them with it as it rotates. Once they have come to this sphere, they recover their vision

D

of divine things. This time, however, they are not
content to reflect them in the dream of a powerless
happiness ; they become impregnated thereby with
the lucidity of a grief-enlightened consciousness,
the energy of a will acquired through struggle and
strife. They become luminous, for they possess the
divine in themselves and radiate it in their acts.
Strengthen therefore thy soul, O Hermes ! calm
thy darkened mind by contemplating these distant
flights of souls which mount the seven spheres and
are scattered about therein like sheaves of sparks.
Thou also canst follow them, but a strong will it
needs to rise. Look how they swarm and form into
divine choruses. Each places itself beneath its
favourite Genius. The most beautiful dwell in the
solar region ; the most powerful rise to Saturn.
Some ascend to the Father, powers themselves
amidst the powers. For where everything ends,
everything eternally begins ; and the seven spheres
say together : ' Wisdom ! Love ! Justice ! Beauty !
Splendour ! Knowledge ! Immortality ! ' "

"This," said the hierophant, "is what ancient
Hermes saw and what his successors have handed
down to us. The words of the wise are like the
seven notes of the lyre which contain all music,
along with the numbers and the laws of the universe.
The vision of Hermes resembles the starry heaven,

whose unfathomable depths are strewn with constellations. For the child this is nothing more than
a gold-studded vault, for the sage it is boundless
space in which worlds revolve, with their wonderful
rhythms and cadences. This vision contains the
eternal numbers, evoking signs and magic keys.
The more thou learnest to contemplate and understand it, the farther thou shalt see its limits extend,
for the same organic law governs all worlds."

The prophet of the temple commented on the
sacred text. He explained that the doctrine of
the Word-Light represents divinity *in the static
condition*, in its perfect balance. He showed its
triple nature, which is at once intelligence, force,
and matter; spirit, soul, and body; light, word,
and life. Essence, manifestation, and substance are
three terms which take each other for granted.
Their union constitutes the divine and intellectual
principle *par excellence*, the law of the ternary unity
which governs creation from above downwards.

Having thus led his disciple to the ideal centre
of the universe, the generating principle of Being,
the master spread him abroad in time and space
in a multiple efflorescence. For the second part of
the vision represents divinity *in the dynamic condition, i.e.* in active evolution; in other terms, the
visible and invisible universe, the living heavens.

The seven spheres attached to the seven planets symbolise seven principles, seven different states of matter and spirit, seven different worlds which each man and each humanity are forced to pass through in their evolution across a solar system. The seven Genii or the seven cosmogonic Gods signify the superior, directing spirits of all spheres, the offspring themselves of inevitable evolution. To an initiate of old, therefore, each great God was the symbol and patron of legions of spirits which reproduced his type in a thousand varieties, and which, from their own sphere, could exercise their action over mankind and terrestrial things. The seven Genii of the vision of Hermes are the seven Devas of India, the seven Amshapands of Persia, the seven great Angels of Chaldæa, the seven Sephiroths [1] of the Kabbala, the seven Archangels of the Christian Apocalypse. The great septenary which enfolds the universe does not vibrate in the seven colours of the rainbow and the seven notes of the scale, only; it also manifests itself in the constitution of man, which is triple in essence, but sevenfold in its evolution. [2]

[1] There are ten Sephiroths in the Kabbala. The first three represent the divine ternary, the seven others the evolution of the universe.

[2] We will here give the Egyptian terms of this septenary constitution of man, found in the Kabbala : *Chat*, material body ; *Anch*, vital force ; *Kan*, etheric double or astral body ; *Hati*,

" Thus," said the hierophant in conclusion, " thou
hast reached the very threshold of the great arcanum.
The divine life has appeared to thee beneath the
phantoms of reality.   Hermes has unfolded to thee
the invisible heavens, the light of Osiris, the hidden
God of the universe who breathes in millions of
souls and animates thereby the wandering globes
and working bodies.   It is now thine to direct thy
path and choose the road leading to the pure
Spirit.   Henceforth dost thou belong *to those who
have been brought back from death to life.*   Remember
that there are two main keys to knowledge.   This
is the first : " The without is like the within of
things ; the small is like the large ; there is only
one law and he who works is One.   In the divine
economy, there is nothing either great or small."
And this is the second : " Men are mortal gods
and gods are immortal men."   Happy the man
who understands these words, for he holds the key
to all things.   Remember that the law of mystery
veils the great truth.   Total knowledge can be
revealed only to our brethren who have gone

---

animal soul ; *Bai*, rational soul ; *Cheybi*, spiritual soul ; *Kou*,
divine spirit ; correspond to the δαίμονες, ἥρωές or ψυχαι ἀχραντοι
of the Greeks.
  The development of these fundamental ideas of the esoteric
teaching will be found in the book of *Orpheus*, and more
especially in that of *Pythagoras*.

through the same trials as ourselves. Truth must be measured according to intelligence; it must be veiled from the feeble, whom it would madden, and concealed from the wicked, who are capable of seizing only its fragments, which they would turn into weapons of destruction. Keep it in thy heart and let it speak through thy work. Knowledge will be thy might, faith thy sword, and silence thy armour that cannot be broken."

The revelations of the prophet of Ammon-Rā, which opened out to the new initiate such vast horizons over himself and over the universe, doubtless produced a profound impression, when uttered from the observatory of a Theban temple, in the clear calm of an Egyptian night. The pylons, the white roofs and terraces of the temples lay asleep at his feet between the dark clusters of nopals and tamarind trees. Away in the distance were large monolithic shrines, colossal statues of the gods, seated like incorruptible judges on their silent lake. Three pyramids, geometrical figures of the tetragram and of the sacred septenary, could be dimly seen on the horizon, their triangles clearly outlined in the light grey air. The unfathomable firmament was studded with stars. With what a strange gaze he looked at those constellations which were depicted to him as future dwellings! When finally the gold-

tipped barque of the moon rose above the dark
mirror of the Nile which died away on the horizon,
like a long bluish serpent, the neophyte believed
he saw the barque of Isis floating over the river
of souls which it carries off towards the sun of
Osiris. He remembered *the Book of the Dead*, and
the meaning of all the symbols was now unveiled
to his mind after what he had seen and learned ;
he might believe himself to be in the crepuscular
kingdom of the Amenti, the mysterious interregnum
between the earthly and the heavenly life, where
the departed, who are at first without eyes and
power of utterance, by degrees regain sight and
voice. He too was about to undertake the great
journey, the journey of the infinite, through worlds
and existences. Hermes had already absolved him
and judged him to be worthy. He had given him
the explanation of the great enigma : " One only
soul, the great soul of the All, by dividing itself
out, has given birth to all the souls that struggle
throughout the universe." Armed with the mighty
secret, he entered the barque of Isis. Rising aloft
into the ether, it floated in the interstellar regions.
The broad rays of a far-spreading dawn were
already piercing the azure veils of the celestial
horizons, and the choir of the glorious spirits, the
Akhimou-Sekou, who have attained to eternal

repose, was chanting: "Rise, Rā Hermakouti, Sun of spirits! Those in thy barque are in exaltation. They raise exclamations in *the barque of millions of years*. The great divine cycle overflows with joy when glorifying the mighty sacred barque. Rejoicing is taking place in the mysterious chapel. Rise, Ammon-Rā Hermakouti, thou self-creating Sun!" And the initiate replied proudly: "I have attained the country of truth and justification. I rise from the dead as a living God, and shine forth in the choir of the Gods who dwell in heaven, for I belong to their race."

Such audacious thoughts and hopes might haunt the spirit of the adept during the night following the mystic ceremony of resurrection. The following morning, in the avenues of the temple, beneath the blinding light, that night seemed to him no more than a dream . . . though how impossible to forget . . . that first voyage into the intangible and invisible! Once again he read the inscription on the statue of Isis: "My veil no mortal hand hath raised." All the same a corner of the veil was raised, but only to fall back again, and he woke up on the earth of tombs. Ah, how far he was from the goal he had dreamed of! For the voyage on *the barque of millions of years* is a long one! But at least he had caught a faint glimpse of his

final destination. Even though his vision of the
other world were only a dream, a childish outline
of his imagination, still obscured by the mists of
earth, could he doubt that other consciousness he
had felt being born in him, that mysterious *double*,
that celestial ego which had appeared to him in its
astral beauty like a living form and spoken to him
in his sleep? Was this a sister-soul, was it his
Genius, or only a reflection of his inmost spirit, a
vision of his future being dimly foreshadowed? A
wonder and a mystery! Surely it was a reality,
and if that soul was only his own, it was the true
one. What would he not do to recover it? Were
he to live millions of years he would never forget
that divine hour in which he had seen his other
self, so pure and radiant.[1]

The initiation was at an end, and the adept
consecrated as priest of Osiris. If he was an
Egyptian, he remained attached to the temple; if
a foreigner, he was permitted, from time to time,
to return to his own country, therein to establish
the worship of Isis or to accomplish a mission.

---

[1] In the Egyptian teachings, man was considered in this life
to have consciousness only of the animal and the rational soul,
called *hati* and *baï*. The higher part of his being, the spiritual
soul and the divine being, *cheybi* and *kou*, exist in him as un-
conscious germs and develop after this life, when he becomes
himself *an Osiris*.

Before leaving, however, he swore a formidable oath that he would maintain absolute silence regarding the secrets of the temple. Never would he betray to a single person what he had seen or heard, never would he reveal the doctrine of Osiris except under the triple veil of the mythological symbols or of the mysteries. Were he to violate this oath, sudden death would come to him, sooner or later, however far away he might be. Silence, however, had become the buckler of his might.

On returning to the shores of Ionia, to the turbulent town in which he formerly lived, amidst that multitude of men, a prey to mad passions, who exist like fools in their ignorance of themselves, his thoughts often flew back to Egypt and the pyramids, to the temple of Ammon-Rā. Then the dream of the crypt came back to memory. And just as the lotus, in that distant land, spreads out its petals on the waves of the Nile, so this white vision floated above the slimy, turbulent stream of this life. At chosen hours, he would hear *its* voice, and it was the voice of light. Arousing throughout his being the strains of an inner music, it said to him: " The soul is a veiled light. When neglected, it flickers and dies out, but when it is fed with the holy oil of love, it shines forth like an immortal lamp."

CPSIA information can be obtained
at www.ICGtesting.com
Printed in the USA
LVHW050924261222
735917LV00011B/1188